Excellent English

Helen Cooper

Wizard Whimstaff lives in a faraway land, in a magical cave. He searches for apprentices so he can pass on his powerful English spells. And this time Wizard Whimstaff has chosen you!

He has a goblin helper called Pointy, who is very clever. Pointy helps Wizard Whimstaff keep his spell books tidy. He also stirs the smelly cauldron to make words appear.

Pointy has two pet frogs called Mugly and Bugly. They are very lazy. They spend most of their time eating, burping and sleeping. Their friend Miss Snufflebeam also lives in the cave. She is a small dragon. She cannot breathe fire yet, so puffs little clouds of smoke instead!

Wizard Whimstaff and his friends are very happy, solving English problems. Join them on a magical quest to win the Trophy of English Wizardry!

Contents

Spooky Sentences

Hello, I am Miss Snufflebeam and I get a little bit confused! **Sentences** need to make sense when we read them, so I must try hard not to mix things up! All of the words must be in the **right order** so that we understand what we are reading.

✘	✔
always hungry are Mugly and Bugly.	Mugly and Bugly are always hungry.
This sentence is muddled up.	This sentence is in the right order.

Task 1 Oh no! I have dropped some words! Can you help me put them back in the right sentences?

computer	market	owls	spin

a We go to the _____ to buy food.

b At night _____ fly around.

c Spiders _____ webs very quickly.

d I like playing on my _____.

Task 2 These are a bit difficult for me. Can you put these words into the right order to make sentences?

a star. a I saw shooting Yesterday

_____

b going Tomorrow camping. are we

_____

2

Task 3 Oh dear! The endings for these sentences have got in a muddle! Help me join up the right endings so the sentences make sense. The first one has been done for us.

a	When it is raining	Wizard Whimstaff's helper.
b	Magic potions are	is a magic word.
c	Apples and oranges	I use my umbrella.
d	Pointy is	to play chess.
e	Abracadabra	are my favourite fruits.
f	I am learning	kept in special bottles.

Sorcerer's Skill Check

Cabracababa! Let me see what you know about sentences! Put a tick in the star next to the sentence if it makes sense. Put a cross in the star if it does not.

a Pointy helps Wizard Whimstaff.

b Mugly are frogs and Bugly.

c went in a train.

d A rocket can fly very fast.

You have done well, my apprentice. You can add a silver shield to your trophy at the back of the book!

Silly Capitals & Full Stops

I am Pointy,
Wizard Whimstaff's assistant!
Let me tell you what I know about
capital letters and full stops.
We use capital letters for people's names,
days of the week, months of the year and
names of places. We also use a capital letter
to start a sentence and a full stop to finish it.

<u>S</u>usan and <u>H</u>elen go up to
<u>L</u>ondon every <u>S</u>aturday in <u>J</u>uly<u>.</u>

Task 1 Practice makes perfect! Some of these sentences do not use
capital letters correctly. Put a tick (✓) in the star if the sentence
is correct.

a Spiders spin webs.

b Every saturday pointy goes to spell classes.

c mugly and bugly do not want to do any work.

d My Uncle Bob has a new job.

e My cousins live in Birmingham.

Task 2 Put the missing full stops in these pairs of sentences. I have
shown you how to do the first one. Now you have a try!

a Pointy is clever. He likes learning new things.

b I have a new coat It is black

c The spell was bubbling in the pot It was very hot

d In the morning I get out of bed I put on my clothes

4

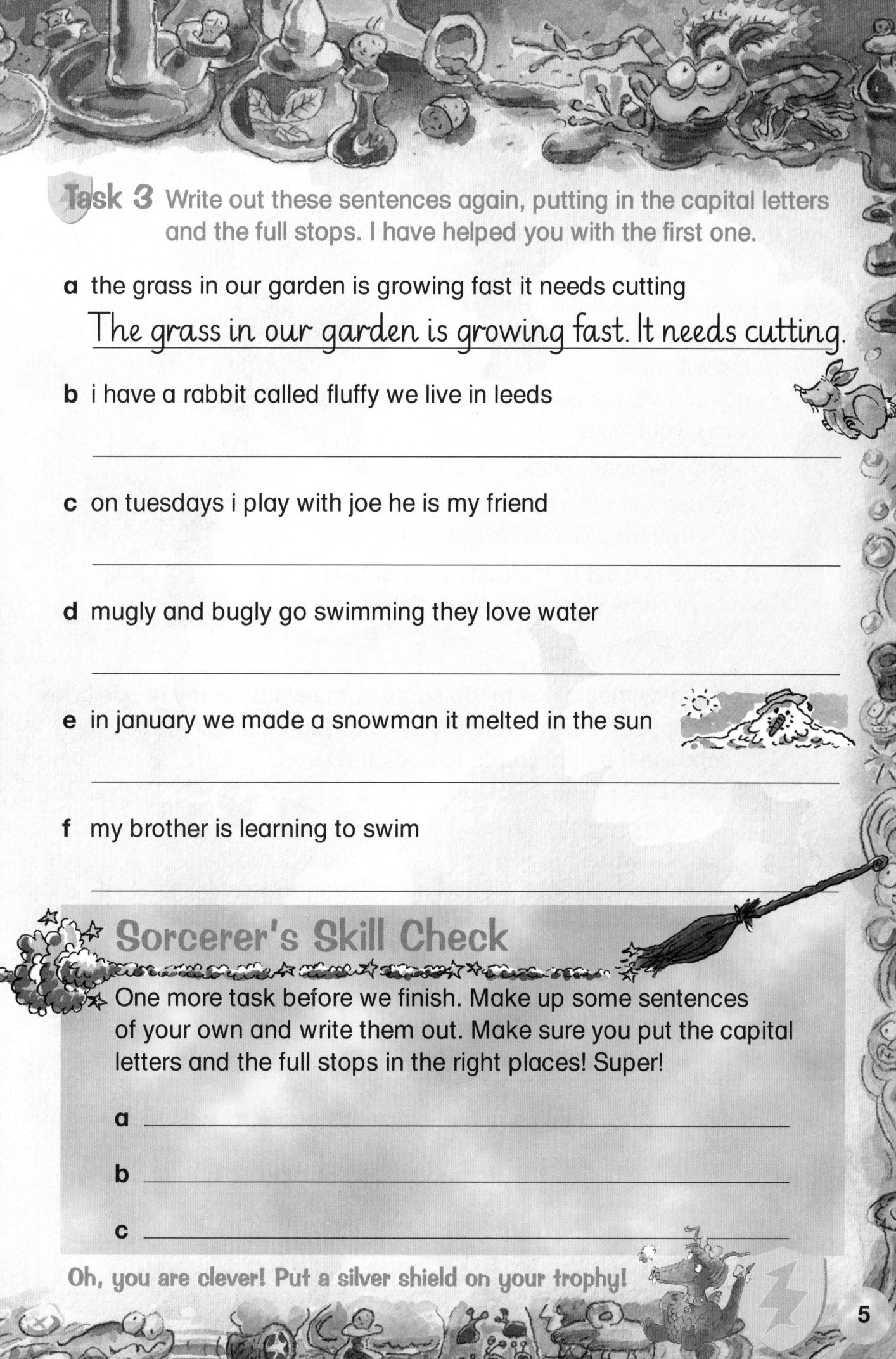

Task 3 Write out these sentences again, putting in the capital letters and the full stops. I have helped you with the first one.

a the grass in our garden is growing fast it needs cutting

The grass in our garden is growing fast. It needs cutting.

b i have a rabbit called fluffy we live in leeds

_____

c on tuesdays i play with joe he is my friend

_____

d mugly and bugly go swimming they love water

_____

e in january we made a snowman it melted in the sun

_____

f my brother is learning to swim

_____

Sorcerer's Skill Check

One more task before we finish. Make up some sentences of your own and write them out. Make sure you put the capital letters and the full stops in the right places! Super!

a _____

b _____

c _____

Oh, you are clever! Put a silver shield on your trophy!

5

Intriguing Instructions

I'm Wizard Whimstaff and I'm good at writing **instructions** for my spells.

- Instructions explain how to do something.
- Instructions often start with a **list** of things you will need.
- Instructions are given in the **correct order**, using words like:

    first   second   next   then   finally

We use instructions all the time in our everyday lives. For example:

A recipe is a set of instructions that tells you how to make a food dish.

Task 1 Clumsy magic has made some of the words in my recipe book disappear! First look at my Wizard Soup ingredients list, then choose the right words to cook the soup.

<u>Wizard Soup</u>
water
goblin sausages

raven's feather
dragon's scale

Choose from these words: Then   First   Finally   Next

a _____ boil the water in the cauldron.

b _____ add some goblin sausages and a raven's feather.

c _____ cut up the dragon's scale and put it in the cauldron.

d _____ give it a stir and serve hot.

Task 2 Now write your own instructions here for making a magic spell. Do not forget to start with a list of ingredients and do not worry if it seems hard at first. My magic will help you! Hey presto!

Ingredients	Instructions
_____	_____
_____	_____
_____	_____
_____	_____
_____	_____

Sorcerer's Skill Check

Now use your magic to rewrite these instructions in the correct order.

> Finally add milk and sugar if needed.
> Then put the boiling water into the cup.
> First put the kettle on to boil.
> Next put the coffee into the cup.

a _____

b _____

c _____

d _____

Slurp! Good work, clever clogs. Give yourself a silver shield.

Scary Synonyms

Burp!
We are Mugly and Bugly, the lazy frogs. We love eating and sleeping but do not like to work. Can you help us? We are looking for words that mean the same thing. They are called synonyms.

sleeping   snoozing   dozing

Find some synonyms for us while we have a little sleep, snooze or doze!

Task 1 Croak! Match the pairs of words that mean the same. Wake us up when you have finished.

a scared   b scream   c cauldron   d brush   e cape

yell   broom   cloak   pot   frightened

Task 2 Slurp! Sort the words that mean the same into pairs. We will carry on dozing.

laugh   eat   replied   leap   munch   jump   stir   stroll
gloomy   walk   sleep   chuckle   answered   mix   sad   nap

a ___sad___ ___gloomy___   e _____ _____

b _____ _____   f _____ _____

c _____ _____   g _____ _____

d _____ _____   h _____ _____

8

Task 3 Put a circle around the word that does not mean the same as the other two words. Grub's up!

a happy   glad   (angry)   **d** stink   pong   taste

b give   grab   snatch   **e** chew   throw   munch

c want   dislike   wish   **f** climb   slip   slide

Task 4 Slurp! Choose a word of your own that means the same as each of these words.

a cross   _____   **d** look   _____

b grin   _____   **e** said   _____

c twinkle   _____   **f** beautiful   _____

Sorcerer's Skill Check

Brain cell alert! One more thing before you can have a good snooze too. Choose another verb that means the same as the verb in each sentence.

| slurped | put | sleep | gobbled |

a I ate my dinner very quickly.   _gobbled_

b I drank some juice at breakfast time.   _____

c The man placed the letter in the box.   _____

d Mugly and Bugly want to doze.   _____

Practice made perfect! Put a silver shield on your trophy!

9

Creepy Commas

Hello,
it is Pointy again!
I want to tell you what I know about commas. We use commas to make lists. They separate a list to make it easier to read, but we have to put them in the right place!

A bug, a slug, a snail and a puppy dog's tail. Did you see that I did not put a comma before the word <u>and</u>? You need to remember that!

Task 1 Now you have a try. Put the missing commas in these lists. You will soon get the hang of it!

a An apple **,** a banana **,** an orange and a pear.

b A potato a carrot an onion and a turnip.

c A car a bus a train and an aeroplane.

d A toad a newt a frog and a pond.

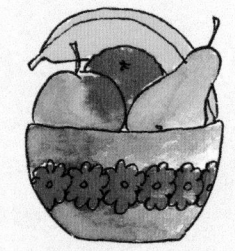

Task 2 These sentences have lists in them. Put the missing commas in the right places. It is easy when you know how!

a Wizard Whimstaff lives with Pointy **,** Miss Snufflebeam **,** Mugly and Bugly.

b The spell room was full of steam smoke smells and noise.

c I love to eat cake sweets chocolate and crisps.

d My favourite colours are red black green and purple.

Task 3 Practice makes perfect! There are some spells bubbling in these cauldrons. Can you write a list of the things needed for each spell, in a sentence separated by commas?

a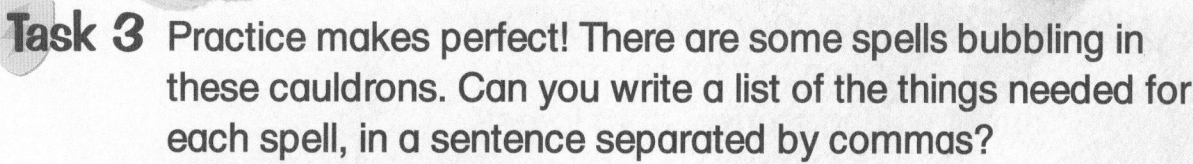

smelly socks   stinky cheese
pongy pants
and a skunk.

To do the smell-killer spell you need

_____

b

wiggly worms   busy bees
creepy caterpillars
and a fly.

To make insect pie you need

_____

Sorcerer's Skill Check

Super! Before you finish, can you make some lists of your own?

a Write a list of things you would put into a vanishing spell.

_____

b Write a list of your favourite animals.

_____

Rabracadada! You will soon be as clever as Pointy!
Have another silver shield.

Sizzling Stories

I am supposed to be telling you about writing **stories**, but I forget which bit is which!

Stories must have a **beginning**, a **middle** and an **end**.

Stories have a **setting**, which means where they take place.

The castle was by the seaside.

Stories have **characters** too.

Pointy likes to help around the castle.

Task 1 I think I remember what a setting is. I have to match these settings to a sentence from their stories, so I hope you will help me!

a   The snow was cold and crunchy under my feet.

b   There was a big hole in the side of the hill. It was dark and cold.

c   The waves were crashing on the sand.

d   The house looked old, empty and scary.

e   I looked on the shelf for a tin of beans and a can of drink.

f   I wanted to go on a fast ride.

the seaside

a cave

a haunted house

a funfair

a snowy mountain

a shop

Task 2 Oh no! I have mixed up these story beginnings and endings. Read them carefully and choose which is a beginning and which is an ending.

beginning   ending

a Once upon a time.

b They all lived happily ever after.

c A funny thing happened on my way home.

d He was never seen again.

Task 3 I am still a bit muddled about beginnings and endings. Can you help me by making some up for me to read?

Write a beginning sentence for a story here.

a _____

Write an ending sentence for a story here.

b _____

Sorcerer's Skill Check

My head hurts because we have worked so hard! Read the word on the left and then put a circle around the word on the right that describes it.

a Miss Snufflebeam is   a setting   a character

b A hospital is   a setting   a character

c A cottage in a wood is   a setting   a character

That was hard. Well completed, young apprentice. Add a silver shield to your trophy!

Apprentice Wizard Challenge 1

Challenge 1 Choose a word from the box to put in each sentence so that it makes sense.

days	lazy	shark	fork

a Mugly and Bugly are two _____ frogs.

b I eat my lunch with a knife and _____.

c Monday and Tuesday are _____ of the week.

d A _____ has very sharp teeth.

Challenge 2 Put the full stops in these sentences and put circles around the words which need capital letters.

a (wizard) (whimstaff) is very clever.

b mum makes lovely curry

c we love going to sheffield to see grandma

d miss snufflebeam wears a green collar

Challenge 3 These instructions are mixed up. Write them out again in the correct order.

Eat your breakfast   **a** _____

Wake up   **b** _____

Go to school   **c** _____

Get washed   **d** _____

Get dressed   **e** _____

Brush your teeth   **f** _____

Challenge 4 Put a circle around the two synonyms in each list.

a (break) (smash) throw   d quick   fast   slip

b silly   clever   stupid   e chilly   hot   cold

c sprint   walk   run   f sweep   wash   brush

Challenge 5 Put the missing commas in these sentences.

a My favourite foods are cheese potatoes apples and bread.

b Pointy put a newt a frog a bat and a spider into the pot.

c I am making a model out of boxes cartons and bottles.

d In winter I wear a hat scarf gloves and a coat.

e In PE lessons we run hop skip and jump.

f The stars were twinkling red orange yellow and purple.

Challenge 6 Read these sentences and choose if they are about a character or a setting. Write **c** for character or **s** for setting in each star.

a The old lady was wearing a black dress.

b The grass was green and juicy.

c The man had a long, sad face.

d The castle walls were tall and thick.

e He was crying and shouting.

6

5

4

3

2

1

Challenge Score

Count how many challenges you got right and put stars on the test tube to show your score. Then have a silver shield for your trophy!

15

Dastardly Dictionaries

I am here to help you find out about new things. I use a dictionary to find out about new words. All the words in a dictionary are in alphabetical order to help you find them easily. The words

elephant ant camel

become ant camel elephant

when you put them in alphabetical order.

A dictionary tells you what a word means. This is called a definition.

Task 1 Now have a go at this exercise. Put these words in alphabetical order. Allakazan!

a blue red green yellow   *blue green red yellow*

b horse sheep cow pig   _____

c toad newt spider bat   _____

d cape hat wand broomstick   _____

e car bus train aeroplane   _____

Task 2 Abracadabra is a magic word. Can you find the definitions of each of these words?

a An apple is   an object that a wizard flies on.

b A wand is   an object with four legs that you sit on.

c A chair is   a round green fruit.

d A broomstick is   a magic stick used by a wizard.

Task 3 Hey Presto! I have mixed up the words in these spellbooks.
Put the words into alphabetical order. Just do the best you can!
I have done the first one for you.

a

pond
frog
croak
lily
water

croak
frog
lily
pond
water

b

TV
radio
video
camera
film

_____
_____
_____
_____
_____

c

lion
monkey
zebra
giraffe
hyena

_____
_____
_____
_____
_____

d

cup
dish
plate
saucer
glass

_____
_____
_____
_____
_____

Sorcerer's Skill Check

Now choose the correct word to match each definition.

lily pad	spell	bed	cup

a a place where you sleep   bed

b the leaf of a plant found in a pond   _____

c something that you drink from   _____

d magic words said by a wizard   _____

You did not get mixed up at all! Give yourself a
silver shield.

Funny Phonemes

Remember us? We are Mugly and Bugly, the lazy frogs. We love making croaking sounds. A phoneme is the name for a sound in a word. Careful though – some phonemes sound the same but are spelt differently!

<u>ow</u> as in cow and <u>ou</u> as in loud

<u>oy</u> as in toy and <u>oi</u> as in oil

<u>air</u> as in hair, <u>ear</u> as in bear and <u>are</u> as in care

Task 1 Croak! Choose the correct phoneme for each word. Is it time for a snack yet?

ow   **ou**

a We saw an __ow__l in our garden.

b There are lots of rain cl_____ds in the sky.

c Wizard Whimstaff has magical p_____er.

d Miss Snufflebeam can breathe fire _____t of her mouth.

e The girl began to scream and sh_____t l_____dly.

f The boy tripped and fell d_____n.

g I went to t_____n to buy some new br_____n shoes.

Task 2 You seem a clever sort of person. You can do this task for us, our grub's ready now! Write each word in the correct place.

hair scared wear lair dare air pear bear stare

containing **air**

_____

_____

_____

containing **ear**

_____

_____

_____

containing **are**

_____

_____

_____

Task 3 Slurp! Sort these **oy** and **oi** words into two sets. Wake us up when you have finished.

toy cowboy soil boy spoil foil ploy coin

oy words

toy _____

_____ _____

oi words

coin _____

_____ _____

Sorcerer's Skill Check

Brain cell alert! One more thing to do, then we can all sleep! Choose the correct phoneme for each word.

a I want to find some information ab_____t snakes.

b The Queen is the head of the r_____al family.

c We live in a t_____er block.

Practice made perfect! Take a silver shield for your trophy.

19

Charming Comprehension

Hello, here I am again, Miss Snufflebeam! I love reading but sometimes I get mixed up. When you read, it is important that you understand what you are reading. You can check you understand by answering questions about something you have read. This is called comprehension.

Task 1 Read this passage carefully, then circle true or false for each statement.

Miss Snufflebeam is a red dragon. She lives in a cave with Wizard Whimstaff. She likes to be helpful, but often gets in a muddle. Sometimes she plays with Mugly and Bugly, the frogs. They are very lazy and sometimes she has to wake them up!

a Miss Snufflebeam often gets muddled.	true	false
b Miss Snufflebeam is a dragon.	true	false
c Miss Snufflebeam is green.	true	false
d Mugly and Bugly are cats.	true	false
e Wizard Whimstaff lives in a cave.	true	false
f Mugly and Bugly are lazy.	true	false

Task 2 I have dropped some words and I am not sure where they should go. Help me to put them back in the correct places.

> mixed   Snufflebeam   clever   dragon   goblin   lives

Wizard Whimstaff [_____] with his friends. They are called

Pointy and Miss [_____]. Pointy is a [_____]. Miss

Snufflebeam is a [_____]. Pointy is very [_____]. Miss

Snufflebeam is not very clever and sometimes gets [_____] up.

Task 3 Put a circle around the correct answer for each sentence.

a Wizard Whimstaff lives in a   caravan   castle   (cave)

b Miss Snufflebeam's wings are   pink   yellow   blue

c Mugly and Bugly are   fruit   frogs   freaks

d Pointy is a   ghost   goblin   ghoul

Sorcerer's Skill Check

My head hurts. Can you help me answer these questions? Remember to use capital letters and full stops.

a What is the wizard's name?

_____

b Who does Miss Snufflebeam sometimes have to wake up?

_____

Slurp! Time for a silver shield and a nice long sleep!

Incredible ing

I am going to show you how to use your magic wand to change **verbs**. A verb is an action word. **-ing** is a magic ending that you can add to a verb. Look how I used my wand to add **-ing** to this verb.

Mugly and Bugly sleep.
Mugly and Bugly are sleep<u>ing</u>.

If a verb ends with the letter **e** you have to take the **e** away before you add **-ing**.

bake + ing = bak<u>ing</u>

Task 1 Now find the **-ing** word in each sentence and draw a circle around it.

a The children are buying pizza.

b The skeleton was rattling his bones.

c A lion was roaring loudly.

d A fairy is dancing in the garden.

e My brother loves wearing brightly coloured clothes.

f I love eating tomato soup.

Task 2 Hey Presto! This time I want you to make some **-ing** words by adding **-ing** to the verbs I have given you.

a cook + ing = _cooking_   **d** fly + ing = _____

b drink + ing = _____   **e** wish + ing = _____

c eat + ing = _____   **f** laugh + ing = _____

Task 3 You are doing well! Can you find the correct **-ing** word to put into each of these sentences?

| sprinkling | putting | cutting | making | saying |

a The cook is _____ a fruit salad.

b He is _____ up the fruit.

c He is _____ it in a bowl.

d He is _____ on some sugar.

e He is _____ "Yum, yum".

Task 4 Have a go with your magic wand at zapping the letter **e** before adding **-ing**. Do not worry if it seems hard at first.

a bake + ing = _____   **b** shine + ing = _____

c twinkle + ing = _____   **d** smile + ing = _____

Sorcerer's Skill Check

Good work young apprentice! You have nearly finished. Can you change these verbs into **-ing** words and put them in the right place?

| read | help | make | bake |

Miss Snufflebeam is _____ Wizard Whimstaff. He is _____ a new spell. The wizard is _____ from his spell book. Miss Snufflebeam is _____ some magic cakes.

Super! What brilliant work! You deserve a silver shield to put on your trophy.

Revolting Recounts

I am going to tell you about writing a recount. Super! A recount is like an account but in the past tense. A recount gives information in the order it happened:

I went to Newcastle with my Dad.
First we went to buy shoes.
We looked for trainers.

Task 1 Rewrite these sentences in the past tense. I have done the first one for you. You will soon get the hang of it!

Remember to answer in full sentences beginning with a capital letter and ending with a full stop.

a My mum goes to work.

My mum went to work.

b My brother plays football.

_____

c Wizard Whimstaff makes a spell.

_____

Task 2 Tell me if these sentences are written in the past or present tense. It is easy when you know how!

a I go to the seaside.   present

b I took a bucket and spade.   _____

c I make a sandcastle.   _____

d I played in the sea.   _____

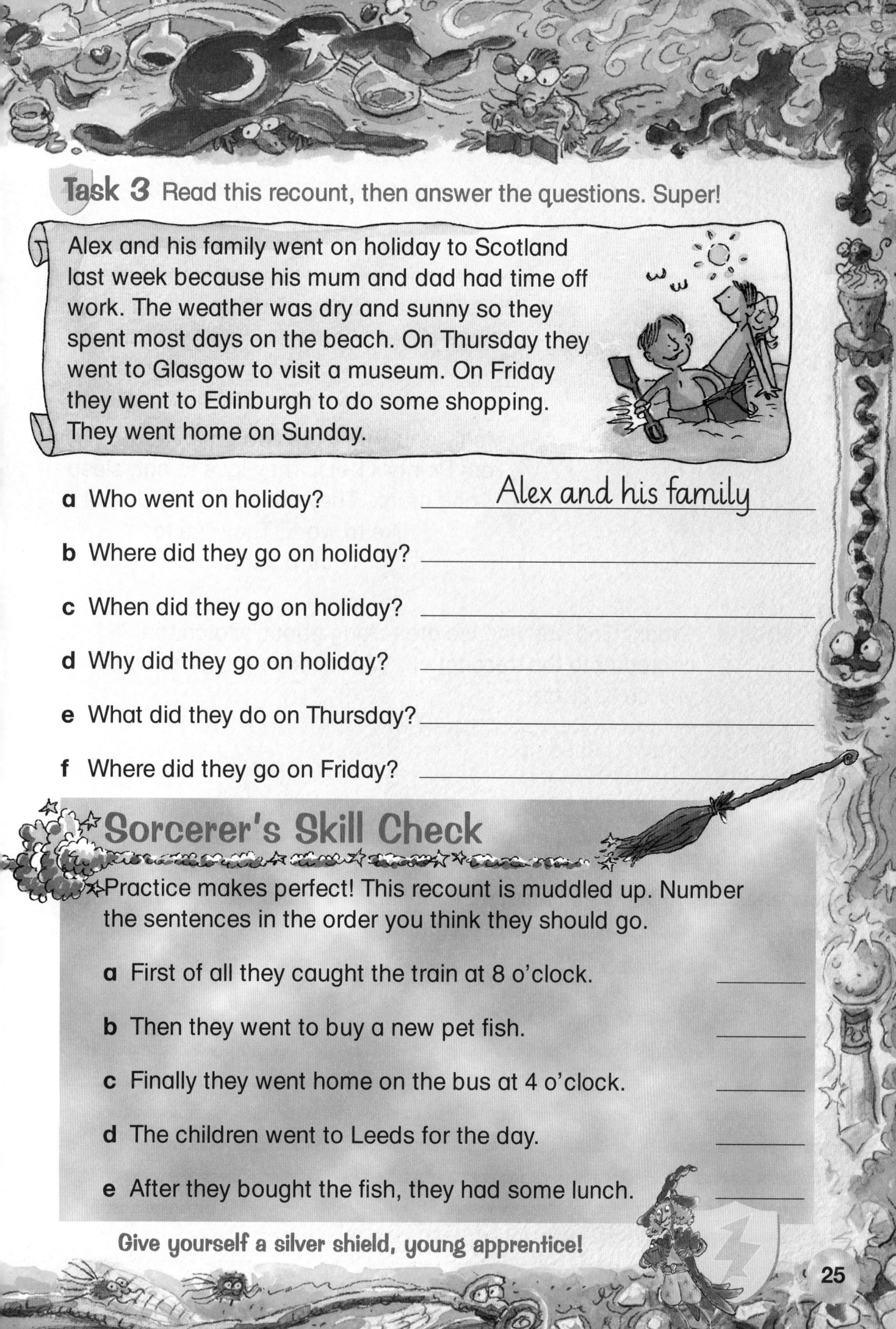

Task 3 Read this recount, then answer the questions. Super!

Alex and his family went on holiday to Scotland last week because his mum and dad had time off work. The weather was dry and sunny so they spent most days on the beach. On Thursday they went to Glasgow to visit a museum. On Friday they went to Edinburgh to do some shopping. They went home on Sunday.

a Who went on holiday? _Alex and his family_

b Where did they go on holiday? _____

c When did they go on holiday? _____

d Why did they go on holiday? _____

e What did they do on Thursday? _____

f Where did they go on Friday? _____

Sorcerer's Skill Check

Practice makes perfect! This recount is muddled up. Number the sentences in the order you think they should go.

a First of all they caught the train at 8 o'clock. _____

b Then they went to buy a new pet fish. _____

c Finally they went home on the bus at 4 o'clock. _____

d The children went to Leeds for the day. _____

e After they bought the fish, they had some lunch. _____

Give yourself a silver shield, young apprentice!

Conjuring Characters

We have been woken up to tell you about **characters**. A character is someone in a story. You can find out lots of things about characters from what they do, what they say and what they look like. Read what has been written about us.

Mugly and Bugly are two green frogs. They are Pointy's pets. They love to eat, sleep and croak. They are lazy. They do not like to work. They like to burp a lot!

Task 1 Croak! Find out who we are talking about. Match the character to the description. We will have a snooze while you do it. Zzzzz...

a She gets muddled up.

b He wears a cape.

c He says "Super!"

d She wears a green collar.

e They are lazy.

f He has a broomstick.

g He helps Wizard Whimstaff.

h They croak.

i She tries to breathe fire.

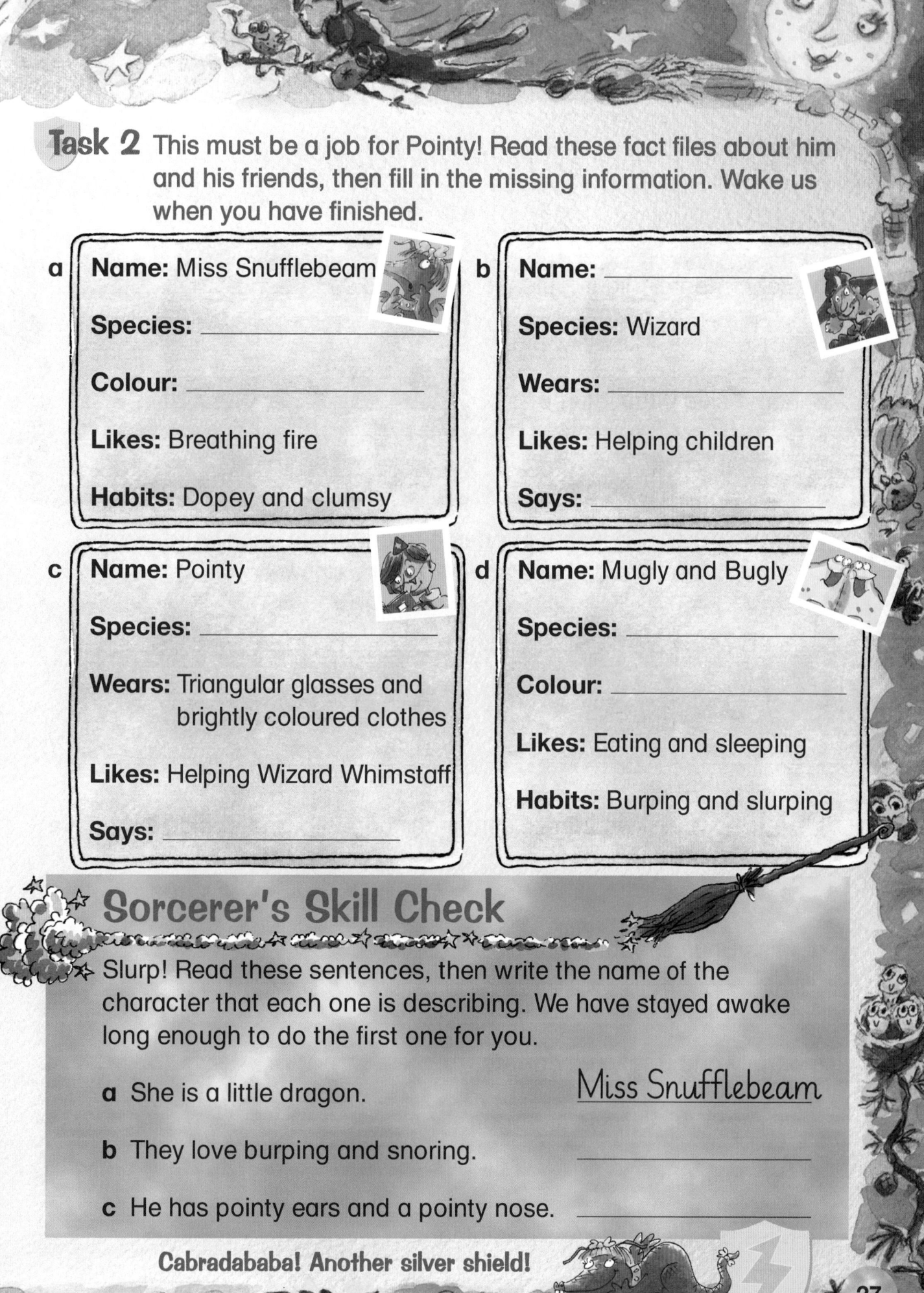

Task 2 This must be a job for Pointy! Read these fact files about him and his friends, then fill in the missing information. Wake us when you have finished.

a
Name: Miss Snufflebeam

Species: _____

Colour: _____

Likes: Breathing fire

Habits: Dopey and clumsy

b
Name: _____

Species: Wizard

Wears: _____

Likes: Helping children

Says: _____

c
Name: Pointy

Species: _____

Wears: Triangular glasses and brightly coloured clothes

Likes: Helping Wizard Whimstaff

Says: _____

d
Name: Mugly and Bugly

Species: _____

Colour: _____

Likes: Eating and sleeping

Habits: Burping and slurping

Sorcerer's Skill Check

Slurp! Read these sentences, then write the name of the character that each one is describing. We have stayed awake long enough to do the first one for you.

a She is a little dragon.   _Miss Snufflebeam_

b They love burping and snoring.   _____

c He has pointy ears and a pointy nose.   _____

Cabradababa! Another silver shield!

Apprentice Wizard Challenge 2

Challenge 1   Put these words in alphabetical order.

a sea   water   river   pond   _____

b star   moon   night   planet   _____

c grass   tree   flower   plant   _____

d hop   skip   run   jump   _____

e wolf   pig   goat   bear   _____

Challenge 2   Choose a phoneme to complete each word. Some
words have more than one answer.

| ou | ow | oy | oi | are | air | ear |

a d_____   **b** f_____l   **c** cl_____n   **d** b_____

e h_____   **f** pr_____d   **g** sc_____

Challenge 3   Read these sentences carefully and decide if they are
true or false.

                                                                  true   false

a Miss Snufflebeam is a dragon.

b Pointy is a goblin.

c Mugly and Bugly are parrots.

d Wizard Whimstaff is a dragon.

e Pointy is lazy.

f Miss Snufflebeam gets muddled up.

Challenge 4 Turn these verbs into **ing** words and put each one into the correct sentence.

> jump   fly   ride   cook

a Mugly and Bugly were ____jumping____ into the water.

b My dad is _____ our dinner.

c A bird is _____ in the sky.

d A cowboy is _____ on his horse.

Challenge 5 Rewrite these sentences in the past tense.

a I wake up.   _____I woke up._____

b I get out of bed.   _____

c I get washed.   _____

Challenge 6 Try to guess the names of these characters.

a I am an animal with sharp teeth. I want to eat the three little pigs.

Who am I? __The big bad wolf.__

b I am a goblin. I help a wizard. I have two pet frogs.

I love finding things out. Who am I? _____

c I live on a ship. I have a parrot. I have a big gold earring.

I look for treasure. Who am I? _____

6

5

4

3

2

1

Challenge Score

Count how many challenges you got right and put stars on the test tube
to show your score. Then take the last silver shield for your trophy!

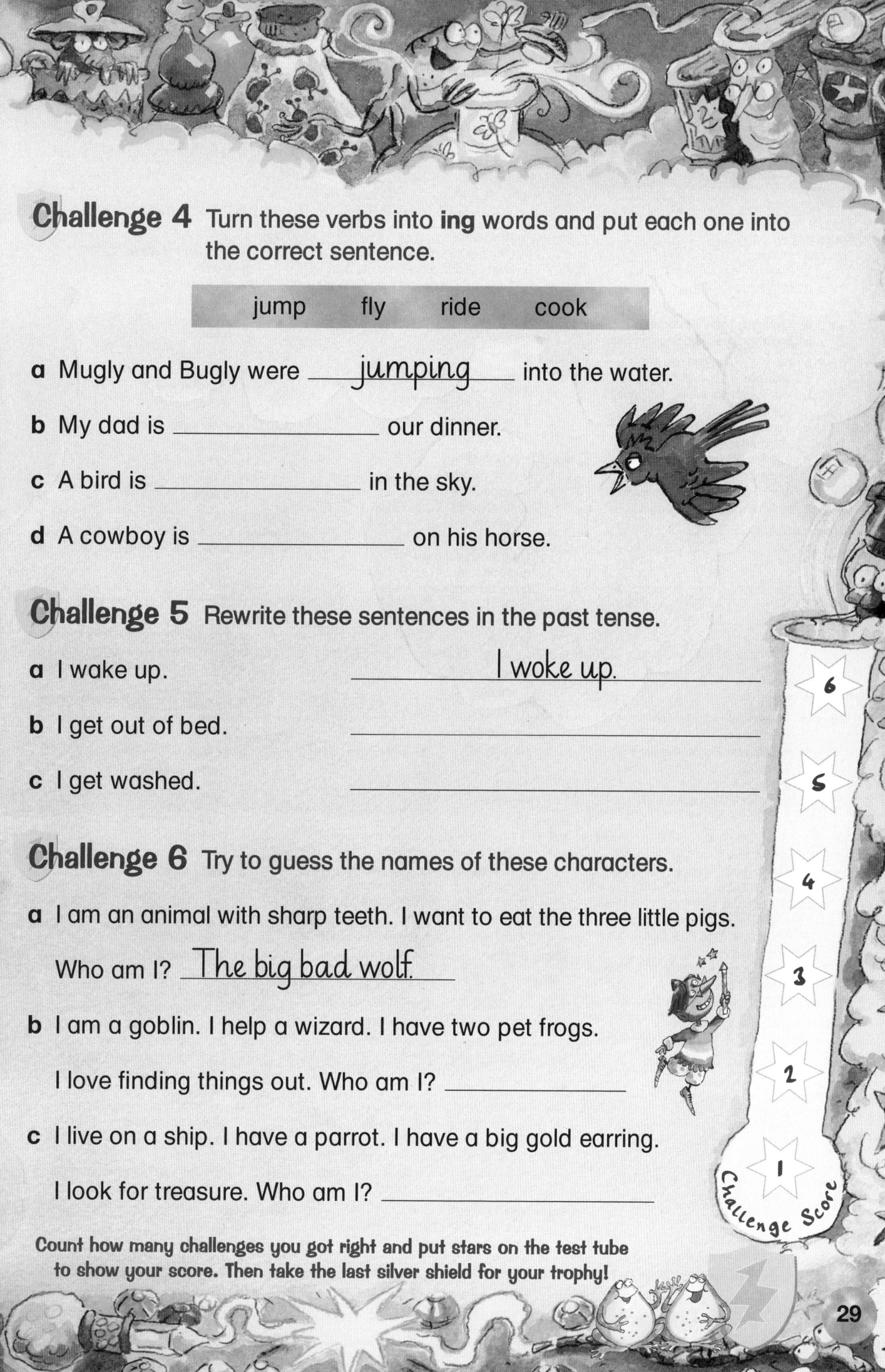

Answers

Pages 2–3

Task 1
a market
b owls
c spin
d computer

Task 2
a Yesterday I saw a shooting star.
b Tomorrow we are going camping.

Task 3
a When it is raining I use my umbrella.
b Magic potions are kept in special bottles.
c Apples and oranges are my favourite fruits.
d Pointy is Wizard Whimstaff's helper.
e Abracadabra is a magic word.
f I am learning to play chess.

Sorcerer's Skill Check
a tick
b cross
c cross
d tick

Pages 4–5

Task 1
a tick
b cross
c cross
d tick
e tick

Task 2
a Pointy is clever. He likes learning new things.
b I have a new coat. It is black.
c The spell was bubbling in the pot. It was very hot.
d In the morning I get out of bed. I put on my clothes.

Task 3
a The grass in our garden is growing fast. It needs cutting.
b I have a rabbit called Fluffy. We live in Leeds.
c On Tuesdays I play with Joe. He is my friend.
d Mugly and Bugly go swimming. They love water.
e In January we made a snowman. It melted in the sun.
f My brother is learning to swim.

Sorcerer's Skill Check
Any sentences using capital letters and full stops correctly are acceptable.

Pages 6–7

Task 1
a First
b Next or Then. Either is correct.
c Next or Then. Either is correct.
e Finally

Task 2 No set answer for this task. Check that instructions are used correctly.

Sorcerer's Skill Check
a First put the kettle on to boil.
b Next put the coffee into the cup.
c Then put the boiling water into the cup.
d Finally add milk and sugar if needed.

Pages 8–9

Task 1
a scared frightened
b scream yell
c cauldron pot
d brush broom
e cape cloak

Task 2 In any order.
a sad gloomy
b eat munch
c jump leap
d stir mix
e nap sleep
f answered replied
g stroll walk
h laugh chuckle

Task 3
a angry
b give
c dislike
d taste
e throw
f climb

Task 4 A variety of answers are possible.

Sorcerer's Skill Check
a gobbled
b slurped
c put
d sleep

Pages 10–11

Task 1
a An apple, a banana, an orange and a pear.
b A potato, a carrot, an onion and a turnip.
c A car, a bus, a train and an aeroplane.
d A toad, a newt, a frog and a pond.

Task 2
a Wizard Whimstaff lives with Pointy, Miss Snufflebeam, Mugly and Bugly.
b The spell room was full of steam, smoke, smells and noise.
c I love to eat cake, sweets, chocolate and crisps.
d My favourite colours are red, black, green and purple.

Task 3
a To do the smell-killer spell you need smelly socks, stinky cheese, pongy pants and a skunk.
b To make insect pie you need wiggly worms, busy bees, creepy caterpillars, and a fly.

Sorcerer's Skill Check
a, b Any lists of objects using commas correctly are acceptable.

Pages 12–13

Task 1
a a snowy mountain
b a cave
c the seaside
d a haunted house
e a shop
f a funfair

Task 2
a beginning
b ending
c beginning
d ending

Task 3 a, b No set answer.

Sorcerer's Skill Check
a a character
b a setting
c a setting

Pages 14–15

Challenge 1
a lazy
b fork
c days
d shark

Challenge 2
a Wizard Whimstaff is very clever.
b Mum makes lovely curry.
c We love going to Sheffield to see Grandma.
d Miss Snufflebeam wears a green collar.

Challenge 3
a Wake up.
b Brush your teeth.
c Get washed.
d Get dressed.
e Eat your breakfast.
f Go to school.

Challenge 4
a break smash
b silly stupid
c sprint run
d quick fast
e chilly cold
f sweep brush

Challenge 5
a My favourite foods are cheese, potatoes, apples and bread.
b Pointy put a newt, a frog, a bat and a spider into the pot.
c I am making a model out of boxes, cartons and bottles.
d In winter I wear a hat, scarf, gloves and a coat.
e In PE lessons we run, hop, skip and jump.
f The stars were twinkling red, orange, yellow and purple.

Challenge 6
a character
b setting
c character
d setting
e character

Pages 16–17

Task 1
a blue, green, red, yellow
b cow, horse, pig, sheep
c bat, newt, spider, toad
d broomstick, cape, hat, wand
e aeroplane, bus, car, train

Task 2
a An apple is a round green fruit.
b A wand is a magic stick used by a wizard.
c A chair is an object with four legs that you sit on.
d A broomstick is an object that a wizard flies on.

Task 3
a croak, frog, lily, pond, water
b camera, film, radio, TV, video
c giraffe, hyena, lion, monkey, zebra
d cup, dish, glass, plate, saucer

Sorcerer's Skill Check
a bed
b lily pad
c cup
d spell

Pages 18–19

Task 1
a owl
b clouds
c power
d out
e shout loudly
f down
g town, brown

Task 2 air: hair, lair, air
ear: wear, pear, bear
are: scared, dare, stare

Task 3 oy words: toy, cowboy, boy, ploy
oi words: soil, spoil, foil, coin

Sorcerer's Skill Check
a about
b royal
c tower

Pages 20–21

Task 1
a true
b true
c false
d false
e true
f true

Task 2 Wizard Whimstaff lives with his friends. They are called Pointy and Miss Snufflebeam. Pointy is a goblin. Miss Snufflebeam is a dragon. Pointy is very clever. Miss Snufflebeam is not very clever and sometimes she gets mixed up.

Task 3
a cave
b pink
c frogs
d goblin

Sorcerer's Skill Check
The wording of answers may vary, but here are some suggested answers.
a The wizard's name is Wizard Whimstaff.
b Mugly and Bugly.

Pages 22–23

Task 1
a buying
b rattling
c roaring
d dancing
e wearing
f eating

Task 2
a cooking
b drinking
c eating
d flying
e wishing
f laughing

Task 3
a making
b cutting
c putting
d sprinkling
e saying

Task 4
a baking
b shining
c twinkling
d smiling

Sorcerer's Skill Check
Miss Snufflebeam is helping Wizard Whimstaff. He is making a new spell. The wizard is reading from his spell book. Miss Snufflebeam is baking some magic cakes.

Pages 24–25

Task 1
a My mum went to work.
b My brother played football.
c Wizard Whimstaff made a spell.

Task 2
a present
b past
c present
d past

Task 3 The wording may vary but any answer resembling these answers is acceptable.
a Alex and his family
b Scotland
c Last week
d Because Mum and Dad had time off work
e To Glasgow to visit a museum
f To Edinburgh to do some shopping

Sorcerer's Skill Check
a First of all they caught the train at 8 o'clock. (2)
b Then they went to buy a new pet fish. (3)
c Finally they went home on the bus at 4 o'clock. (5)
d The children went to Leeds for the day. (1)
e After they bought the fish, they had some lunch. (4)

Pages 26–27

Task 1
a She gets muddled up = Miss Snufflebeam
b He wears a cape = Wizard Whimstaff
c He says "Super!" = Pointy
d She wears a green collar = Miss Snufflebeam
e They are lazy = Mugly and Bugly
f He has a broomstick = Wizard Whimstaff
g He helps Wizard Whimstaff = Pointy
h They croak = Mugly and Bugly
i She tries to breathe fire = Miss Snufflebeam

Task 2
a The missing words are:
Species = dragon
Colour = red
b The missing words are:
Name = Whimstaff
Wears = cape, hat
Says = Abracadabra, Allakazan (or any other of his catch phrases are acceptable)
c The missing words are:
Species = goblin
Says = Super! (or any other of his catch phrases are acceptable)
d The missing words are:
Species = frogs
Colour = green

Sorcerer's Skill Check
a Miss Snufflebeam
b Mugly and Bugly
c Pointy

Pages 28–29

Challenge 1
a pond river sea water
b moon night planet star
c flower grass plant tree
d hop jump run skip
e bear goat pig wolf

Challenge 2
a dare, dear
b foil, fowl or foul
c clown
d bare, bear, bow, boy
e how, hair, hare, hear
f proud
g scare

Challenge 3
a true
b true
c false
d false
e false
f true

Challenge 4
a jumping
b cooking
c flying
d riding

Challenge 5
a I woke up.
b I got out of bed.
c I got washed.

Challenge 6
a The big bad wolf
b Pointy
c A pirate or Long John Silver

The end

Wizard's Trophy of Excellence

Spooky Sentences

Silly Capitals & Full Stops

Dastardly Dictionaries

Funny Phonemes

Intriguing Instructions

Scary Synonyms

Charming Comprehension

Incredible ing

Creepy Commas

Sizzling Stories

Revolting Recounts

Conjuring Characters

Apprentice Wizard Challenge 1

Apprentice Wizard Challenge 2

This is to state that Wizard Whimstaff awards

Apprentice _____

the Trophy of English Wizardry. Congratulations!

Published 2002
10 9 8 7 6 5 4 3 2

Letts Educational, The Chiswick Centre,
414 Chiswick High Road, London W4 5TF
Tel 020 8996 3333 Fax 020 8742 8390
Email mail@lettsed.co.uk
www.letts-education.com

Text, design and illustrations © Letts Educational Ltd 2002

Author: Helen Cooper
Book Concept and Development:
Helen Jacobs, Publishing Director; Sophie London, Project Editor
Series Editor: Lynn Huggins-Cooper
Design and Editorial: 2idesign ltd, Cambridge
Cover Design: Linda Males
Illustrations: Mike Phillips and Neil Chapman (Beehive Illustration)
Cover Illustration: Neil Chapman

Letts Educational Limited is a division of Granada Learning Limited.
Part of Granada plc.

British Library Cataloguing in Publication Data

A CIP record for this book is available from the British Library.

ISBN 1 84315 118 9

Printed and bound in Italy

Colour reproduction by PDQ Digital Media Solutions Limited,
Bungay, Suffolk.